Goliath Beetles

by Grace Hansen

Abdo
SUPER SPECIES
Kids

abdopublishing.com

Published by Abdo Kids, a division of ABDO, PO Box 398166, Minneapolis, Minnesota 55439.

Copyright © 2017 by Abdo Consulting Group, Inc. International copyrights reserved in all countries. No part of this book may be reproduced in any form without written permission from the publisher.

Printed in the United States of America, North Mankato, Minnesota.

052016

092016

THIS BOOK CONTAINS RECYCLED MATERIALS

Photo Credits: Alamy, Corbis, iStock, Minden Pictures, Science Source, Shutterstock

Production Contributors: Teddy Borth, Jennie Forsberg, Grace Hansen

Design Contributors: Laura Mitchell, Dorothy Toth

Cataloging-in-Publication Data

Names: Hansen, Grace, author.

Title: Goliath beetles / by Grace Hansen.

Description: Minneapolis, MN : Abdo Kids, [2017] | Series: Super species |
    Includes bibliographical references and index.

Identifiers: LCCN 2015959215 | ISBN 9781680805451 (lib. bdg.) |
    ISBN 9781680806014 (ebook) | ISBN 9781680806571 (Read-to-me ebook)

Subjects: LCSH: Goliath beetles--Juvenile literature.

Classification: DDC 595.76--dc23

LC record available at http://lccn.loc.gov/2015959215

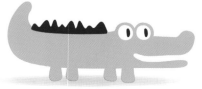

Table of Contents

Big Bugs!

Goliath beetles live in Africa. They are the heaviest beetle **species**. They are also the heaviest insects!

5

Goliath beetles can weigh up to 3.5 ounces (100 g)! An adult robin weighs just 2.7 ounces (77 g).

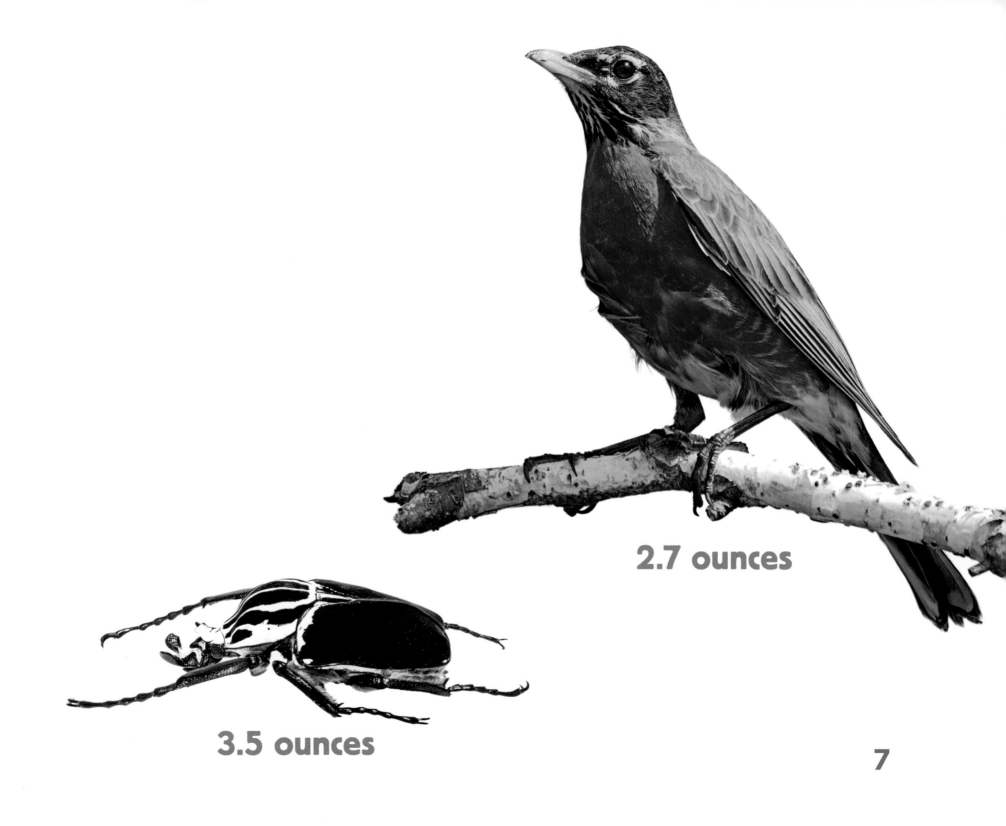

2.7 ounces

3.5 ounces

7

Goliaths can grow up to

4.5 inches (11 cm) long.

That is longer than a

monarch butterfly's wingspan.

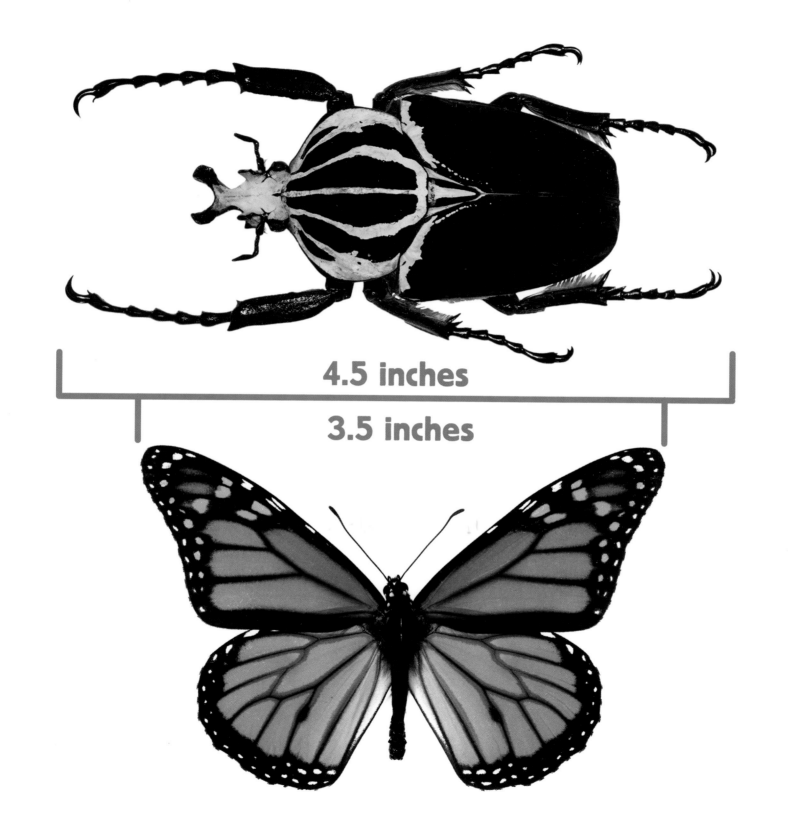

4.5 inches

3.5 inches

Goliath beetles are one of the strongest insects. They can lift up to 850 times their own weight!

Body

Goliaths are usually oval shaped. They come in many colors. But they are often black, brown, and white.

Goliaths have six strong legs. Each leg ends in a sharp claw. This makes them good diggers and climbers.

15

Goliaths have outer wings called **elytra**. Beneath them is a pair of softer wings. The elytra protect the softer wings. The softer wings are used for flying.

Goliaths are strong fliers.

Their wings make a loud sound.

It sounds like a helicopter.

Food

These big bugs are important to the **environment**. They clean up the forest floor. They eat rotting plants and animal remains.

20

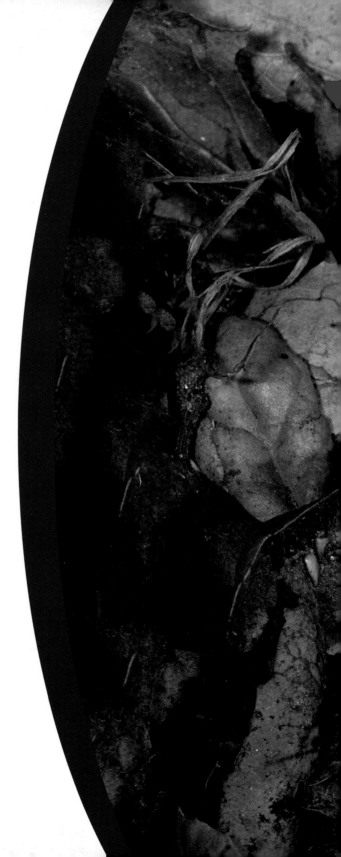

More Facts

- Goliaths love sugar! They also spend most of their time in trees. So, they eat lots of tree sap.

- Goliath beetles can also be purple, green, blue, or gold in color.

- Goliath **larvae** form cocoons that can grow up to 6 inches (15 cm) long!

Glossary

elytra – one of the outer wings on beetles that protect the inner pair of functional wings.

environment – the natural surroundings in which an animal lives.

larvae – active immature insects, especially ones that differ greatly from the adults.

species – a particular group of animals that are similar and can produce young animals.

23

Index

abdokids.com

Use this code to log on to abdokids.com and access crafts, games, videos, and more!

Abdo Kids Code:
SGK5451